Love Speaks

A Pocketful of Poems from Spirit, meditations and a journal sprinkled with timeless words of wisdom to write your own inspired words.

Written by Melinda Maysonet

Balboa Press books may be ordered through booksellers or by contacting:

Balboa Press
A Division of Hay House
1663 Liberty Drive
Bloomington, IN 47403
www.balboapress.com
1 (877) 407-4847

ISBN: 978-1-5043-9576-2 (sc)
ISBN: 978-1-5043-9577-9 (e)

Library of Congress Control Number: 2018900727

Print information available on the last page.

Balboa Press rev. date: 02/07/2018

BALBOA
PRESS
A DIVISION OF HAY HOUSE

Introduction

Welcome and thank you, thank you, thank you for purchasing this book!

These poems would come to me shortly after prayer and meditation. They each came at a time when I needed to hear and believe their messages. I knew it was God/Love/Source/Life/the Universe speaking to me and through me. After writing each poem, I'd read it and be amazed by its simple, yet profound message. I would contemplate each one and feel comforted and encouraged to continue moving forward in spite of fears or doubts. I felt as if my prayers were heard and answered, and I was being reminded of how much I am loved, how amazing and unique I am, and that I have something valuable to share with the world.

I then invite you to let Love speak to you and through you. I've included a few mediations to help you get quiet and listen; and a journal to write the messages you receive during the meditation, sprinkled with some of my favorite quotes full of wisdom from famous personalities that have encouraged me and inspired more than a few "AHA" moments.

My hope is that this book will touch your heart and encourage you along your life's journey.

I wish you many blessings, and remember to dream big and in Technicolor because it's fun, it's free and dreams really can come true. Enjoy your journey!

Melinda

Part I

Poems from Spirit

I Am

Who am I?

I Am

What am I?

I Am

Is that not the name of God?

I Am That I Am

How can I be God?

But I AM!

So be it.

I Am the light of the world.

I Am the door no man can close.

I Am That, I Am!

Today

I serve you Lord.

What would you have me do today?

Where would you have me go today?

Who would you have me speak with today?

And what would you have me say?

I go to be the Light,

I go to show the Love

      to those who may not remember the way.

I Am Light today.

I Am Love today.

I Am You today.

I Am The Way today.

I Knew You When

I knew you when I was young,
    when I was old.
I knew you when it was another time,
    another place,
    another space.
I knew you before the when.
I always knew you.

Come

Come to me
      Sit with me
      Talk with me
      Cry with me
      Laugh with me
      Wonder with me
      Dream with me
      Create with me
Come
I Am always here
      Waiting quietly, patiently
      For you to come to me
Come

Here I Am

Here I Am.

I Am here, are you?

Here I Am, said Moses.

Here I Am, said Samuel.

Here I Am, send me! said Isaiah.

Here I Am.

I Am here, are you?

I Am with you always, said Jesus.

Here I Am.

I Am here, are you?

I Am.

Love

What is Love?
Who is Love?
Love is patient.
Love is kind.
Love never fails.
I Am Love, are you?
I Am patient.
I Am kind.
I Am triumphant!
I Am Love, are you?
I AM!

Impossible

Impossible.
Why?
Why not?
Maybe, perhaps…
All things are possible with God.
Open your mind.
Free your mind.
DREAM!
Dream the impossible,
For all things ARE possible.

I Am Determined to See

I Am determined to see
>   The truth,
>   Who I Am,
>   Why I came,
>   What I Am to do.

I Am determined to see
>   With an unveiled face,
>   With no scales on my eyes,
>   With no scars,
>   Just truth.

I Am determined to see
>   Show me,
>   Enlighten me,
>   Empower me.

I Am determined to see, are you?
I AM!

One

There is only One
>One God
>
>One Universal Consciousness
>
>One Infinite Intelligence
>
>One Life
>
>One Love

There is only One
>One of us here
>
>One of us there
>
>One of us everywhere

There is only One
>We are all One

There is only One!

Fruit

Good fruit.
Ripe fruit.
    Have you any?
Good fruit.
Ripe fruit.
    Love
    Joy
    Peace
    Patience
    Kindness
    Goodness
    Faithfulness
    Gentleness
    Self-control
Good fruit.
Ripe fruit.
    Are you any?
Yes, I AM!

Faith Without Works

Faith without works is dead.
    I am cold.
    I am hungry.
    I am thirsty.
    I am alone.
Never! For I Am here.
    I will clothe you.
    I will feed you.
    I will quench your thirst.
    I will comfort you.
I Am the Light of the world.
Are you?
I AM!

Peace

Peace! Be still!
  I feel afraid.
  I feel lost.
  Where do I go?
  What do I do?
Fear not, for I Am with you.
  I will comfort you.
  I will guide you.
  I will never leave you.
  I AM with you always.
Peace is with me always.
And also with you!

The Light

The Light given by God
    The Light of the sun
    That brightens our days
    That warms our souls
    That brings joy to our hearts
I Am the light of the world, said Jesus
    To brighten your life
    To renew your heart
Follow me, follow my steps
So that you may be a Light, the Light of God
Are you Light?
Yes, I Am!

La Luz

La Luz que Dios nos dio

    La Luz del sol

    Que alumbra los dias

    Que calienta el alma

    Que alegra el corazón

Yo Soy la luz del mundo, dijo Jesus

    Para alumbrarte la vida

    Para renovar tu corazón

Sígueme, sigue mis pasos

Para que seas una Luz, la Luz de Dios

¿Eres Luz?

¡Si, Yo Soy!

I Am Light

Be a Light unto a dark world
      Shine away the darkness
      Expose the fears
      Banish the doubts
Be the Light of the world
      Shine bright with Love
      Love casts out all fear, all doubt, all insecurity
I Am Light, are you?
I Am the light of the world
I Am!

Rest

Give me rest
> Dispel the turmoil
> Dissolve the anger
> Ease the anxiety

Give me rest

Restore my soul to peace and joy

Choose to *BE*
> I Am Rest
> I Am Peace
> I Am Joy

Yes, I Am!

Transformation

Transform, do not conform
        Renew your mind
        Expand your thoughts
        Relinquish dogma
Transform the world
        Imagine
        Create
        Shine bright
Transform into His image
Transform into Love

Show Me

Show me why
Show me how
Show me when
Peace. Be Still. Know that I Am.
I Am Peace
I Am Joy
I Am Love
I Am Life itself, unfolding into limitless possibilities
I Am That, I Am
Are you?
I Am!

I Love Myself

I love myself
I love my big brown eyes
      My bright toothy smile
      My chubby toes
      My not quite magazine model ready body
I deeply and completely love and accept myself
I love life and Life loves me
I love myself for I Am Life itself!
Are you?
I Am!

I Am Home

I Am home, always

I Am home, in my mind

      Where all my memories and dreams live

I Am home, in my heart

      Where all the love I give and receive lives

I Am home, in my soul

      Where Life itself dwells and animates all that is

I Am home, always

      It goes with me wherever I go

      It lives within me

      It is me

I Am home, always

      I Am Life

      Life is Love

      Love is God

      God is Home

I Am home, always

I Am!

He Knows

I don't know
> Where to go
> What to do
> What to say

But…He Knows
He who lights my path
> Orders my steps
> Shows me the way

He who lives in my soul
> And animates my body

He who lives in me, *HE KNOWS*
He who shines the darkness away
I Am the Light that shines
I Am He, He is me
He Who Knows is me!

Life is Just a Thought

What if life is just a thought?

    An idea

    An illusion

    A smoke screen with images

    A nightmare that's frightening

What if I can change it with a new thought?

    A different idea

    A new imagining

        With peaceful and joy filled images

    A happy dream

What if I change my mind?

What if I ponder new thoughts and change my life?

What if Life is just a thought?

The Breeze

Do you feel it?
A soft, cool breeze, a whisper caressing your face, prickling your skin?
Can you feel it?
As if blowing through a large, beautiful bay window with white sheer curtains billowing, overlooking an endless turquoise sea and clear topaz sky.
Do you know it?
It quietly speaks of knowledge and truth, of wisdom and revelation.
The breeze of consciousness.
The breeze of Love revealing itself to you.

I See God

I see blue skies and billowy white clouds
I see the hot fiery sun
I see the glowing moon and twinkling stars
I see God
I see towering trees and beautiful flowers
I see fluttering butterflies and curious insects
I see God
I see majestic mountains and calm lakes
I see roaring seas and white sands
I see God
I see soaring birds and amazing animals
I see God
I see you, I see me
I see God
Do you?

I Belong

Do I belong?
To whom do I belong?
Where do I belong?
I be-long?
Who do I be and for how long?
Oh!
I belong to God.
I belong to Love.
I belong because I Am.
I Am love, loved and loving.
I belong.

I Am What I See

Am I what I see?

What if what I see wounds me?

How can that be?

You don't look like me.

What if I choose to see beauty?

What if I choose to see perfection?

What if I choose to see through compassionate eyes?

What if I choose to see only love?

God is Love.

God is everywhere.

God is in everything and everyone.

I see only Love.

I see you, I see me.

I see Love.

I Am what I see.

I Know I Am

I think I can
Wait…
I know I can
No!
I know I Am
I Am that which I desire
I Am that to which I aspire
I Am those I inspire
I Am That, I Am
I Am all that is, for it is all within me
I Am what I imagine
I Am what I create
I Am That, I Am
I Know I Am!

Bright Light

I see the twinkling of bright lights
  In the distance, afar
Beckoning me to come to them, now!
  Where my dreams are alive
  Waiting for me to join them
I can see glimpses, shimmering, calling to me…
  Take one step, yes! Then another
  One more step, you're so close, keep coming!
OH, but can I? Dare I?
  I must!
For my dreams are within me
  Yearning to come forth
  To be a bright light
  Lighting the way for others
  To take one step, just one
I must
For I am my dreams
I am a bright light
And so are you!

Grace

Here I Am Lord
An empty vessel
Fill me with your divine grace
The grace of faith that can move mountains
      and know all things are possible
The grace of wisdom to know what is best for me
The grace of compassion for my fellow creatures
The grace of forgiveness for myself and others
The grace of courage to move forward in the face of fear
The grace to be of service in this world
Fill me with your divine grace, Lord
The grace of Love
Fill me with You!

The Vessel

I Am an empty vessel, Lord
Fill me to overflowing with

    your grace

    your wisdom

    your holy spirit

Fill me full of peace and joy and knowing
I Am an empty vessel, Lord
Fill me with your light to overflowing

    that I may fill the vessels of others in your service

    fulfilling my journey in this strange land

    completing a life well lived

Part II

Meditations and a journal sprinkled with words of wisdom to write your own inspired words.

Meditation Preparation

Find some place pleasant and quiet where you will not be disturbed. The length of time and whether you prefer to sit or lie down is up to you, do whatever makes you feel most comfortable.

Next, set an intention for your meditation. You can ask for guidance or clarity on a specific situation, or just get quiet, be still and observe your thoughts as they float through your mind. If you find yourself paying too much attention to a specific thought, let it go and focus on your breathing, on the cool air as it comes in through your nostrils and the warm air as it goes out.

Take a few deep breaths in through your nose, filling your lungs and expanding your belly, and let it out through your mouth with a loud sigh. Feel your body release tension and relax. Continue breathing deeply at your own steady pace.

Gently close your eyes and imagine one of the following:

Meditation ~ At the Meadow

You are in a beautiful, serene, picturesque place. It is shortly after sunrise and the sun is warm and shining, not yet too hot or too bright. The sky is clear and blue with a few fluffy white clouds.

You find yourself at an empty lush meadow with soft dewy grass, beautiful colorful flowers and a few tall, strong trees full of leaves rustling quietly with the gentle breeze. You stand there feeling the warmth of the sun on your skin, taking deep breaths and smiling. Imagine that the sun's rays are coating you with a layer of healing light that penetrates the pores on your skin and shines away all dis-ease. Deeply breathe in the crisp and refreshing air rolling in over the hills in the distance.

You feel the breeze gently caressing your skin, it brings with it quiet, barely audible whispers, calling your attention to their messages. Stand there quietly and listen. Observe your thoughts as they float in and out of your mind easily. Listen to the soft whispers on the breeze. What are they saying? What do they want you to know? Just stand there, feeling warm and soothed, listening, taking in the warmth of the sun and breathing in the refreshing air. No need to do anything, just stand there taking it all in, comfortably and effortlessly. Breathing deeply. Listening.

When you feel ready open your eyes, have a good stretch, and write down any words, ideas or impressions you received during the meditation.

Mediation ~ At the Sea Shore

You are in a beautiful, serene, picturesque place. It is shortly after sunrise and the sun is warm and shining, not yet too hot or too bright. The sky is clear and blue with a few fluffy white clouds.

You find yourself at an empty beach with white, sparkly, powdery sand and tall, lush palm trees swaying with the soft breeze; you hear the waves cascading softly against the sand. You stand there feeling the warmth of the sun on your skin, taking deep breaths and smiling. Imagine that the sun's rays are coating you with a layer of healing light that penetrates the pores on your skin and shines away all dis-ease. Deeply breathe in the crisp and refreshing salty air blowing in from the vast, serene, sapphire blue sea.

You feel the breeze gently caressing your skin, it brings with it quiet, barely audible whispers, calling your attention to their messages. Stand there quietly and listen. Observe your thoughts as they float in and out of your mind easily. Listen to the soft whispers on the breeze. What are they saying? What do they want you to know? Just stand there, feeling warm and soothed, listening, taking in the warmth of the sun and breathing in the refreshing air. No need to do anything, just stand there taking it all in, comfortably and effortlessly. Breathing deeply. Listening.

When you feel ready open your eyes, have a good stretch, and write down any words, ideas or impressions you received during the meditation.

Peace is the result of retraining your mind to process life as it is,
rather than as you think it should be. – Wayne Dyer

_____

_____

_____

_____

_____

_____

_____

_____

_____

_____

_____

_____

_____

_____

*Instinct is something which transcends knowledge. We have, undoubtedly,
certain finer fibers that enable us to perceive truths when logical deduction,
or any other willful effort of the brain is futile. – Nikola Tesla*

_____

_____

_____

_____

_____

_____

_____

_____

_____

_____

_____

_____

_____

_____

_____

_____

_____

_____

Your vision will become clear only when you can look into your own heart.
Who looks outside, dreams; who looks inside, awakes. – Carl Jung

_____

_____

_____

_____

_____

_____

_____

_____

_____

_____

_____

_____

_____

_____

_____

_____

_____

I find that when we really love and accept and approve of ourselves
exactly as we are, then everything in life works. – Louise Hay

_____

_____

_____

_____

_____

_____

_____

_____

_____

_____

_____

_____

_____

_____

_____

*Ask and it will be given to you; seek and you will find; knock and the
door will be opened to you. – Jesus, Matthew 7:7 (NIV)*

_____

_____

_____

_____

_____

_____

_____

_____

_____

_____

_____

_____

_____

_____

_____

_____

Attitude is everything, so pick a good one. – Wayne Dyer

_____

_____

_____

_____

_____

_____

_____

_____

_____

_____

_____

_____

_____

_____

_____

The gift of mental power comes from God, Divine Being, and if we concentrate our minds on that truth, we become in tune with this great power. – Nikola Tesla

_____

_____

_____

_____

_____

_____

_____

_____

_____

_____

_____

_____

_____

_____

The shoe that fits one person pinches another; there is no recipe for living that suits all cases. – Carl Jung

_____

_____

_____

_____

_____

_____

_____

_____

_____

_____

_____

_____

_____

_____

_____

Every thought we think is creating our future. – Louise Hay

_____

_____

_____

_____

_____

_____

_____

_____

_____

_____

_____

_____

_____

Jesus said, "Let the little children come to me, and do not hinder them, for the kingdom of heaven belongs to such as these." Matthew 19:14 (NIV)

_____

_____

_____

_____

_____

_____

_____

_____

_____

_____

_____

_____

_____

_____

_____

_____

When you stay on purpose and refuse to be discouraged by fear, you align
with the infinite self, in which all possibilities exist. – Wayne Dyer

_____

_____

_____

_____

_____

_____

_____

_____

_____

_____

_____

_____

_____

_____

Be alone, that is the secret of invention; be alone, that is when ideas are born. – Nikola Tesla

---

Dreams are the guiding words of the soul. Why should I henceforth not love my dreams and not make their riddling images into objects of my daily consideration? – Carl Jung

_____

_____

_____

_____

_____

_____

_____

_____

_____

_____

_____

_____

_____

_____

_____

Work on doing what is right for you and getting in touch with your own inner voice. Your inner wisdom knows the right answers for you. – Louise Hay

_____

_____

_____

_____

_____

_____

_____

_____

_____

_____

_____

_____

_____

_____

_____

_____

Jesus looked at them and said, "With man this is impossible, but with God all things are possible." Matthew 19:26 (NIV)

_____

_____

_____

_____

_____

_____

_____

_____

_____

_____

_____

_____

_____

_____

Doing what you love is the cornerstone of having abundance in your life. – Wayne Dyer

_____

_____

_____

_____

_____

_____

_____

_____

_____

_____

_____

_____

_____

_____

_____

I do not think there is any thrill that can go through the human heart like that felt by the inventor as he sees some creation of the brain unfolding to success. Such emotions make a man forget food, sleep, friends, love, everything. – Nikola Tesla

_____

_____

_____

_____

_____

_____

_____

_____

_____

_____

_____

_____

_____

_____

_____

All the works of man have their origin in creative fantasy. What right have we then to depreciate imagination. – Carl Jung

I trust my intuition. I am willing to listen to that still, small voice within. – Louise Hay

_____

_____

_____

_____

_____

_____

_____

_____

_____

_____

_____

_____

_____

Therefore I tell you, whatever you ask for in prayer, believe that you have received it, and it will be yours. – Jesus, Mark 11:24 (NIV)

_____

_____

_____

_____

_____

_____

_____

_____

_____

_____

_____

_____

_____

_____

_____

_____

Miracles come in moments. Be ready and willing. – Wayne Dyer

If you want to find the secrets of the universe, think in terms of energy, frequency and vibration. – Nikola Tesla

Without this playing with fantasy no creative work has ever yet come to birth. The debt we owe to the play of imagination is incalculable. – Carl Jung

_____

_____

_____

_____

_____

_____

_____

_____

_____

_____

_____

_____

_____

_____

I let the light of my love shine. – Louise Hay

_____

_____

_____

_____

_____

_____

_____

_____

_____

_____

_____

_____

_____

_____

_____

Believe me when I say that I am in the Father and the Father is in me; or at least believe on the evidence of the works themselves. Very truly I tell you, whoever believes in me will do the works I have been doing, and they will do even greater things than these, because I am going to the Father. – Jesus, John 14:11-12 (NIV)

About the Author

"Success is helping others succeed."

Melinda has a private practice offering intuition development, psychic mediumship, leadership coaching and personal consulting. In conjunction with her studies and experiences gained under the tutelage of great leaders, she is able to be of service to others through the contemplation and application of psychological, philosophical, spiritual, metaphysical and coaching principles. She is passionate about helping people connect to and cultivate a relationship with their intuition so they can realize their greatest potential and pursue their wildest dreams. For more information and to connect with Melinda, visit MelindaMaysonet.com.

About the Illustrator

"Leaving love, peace and happiness in my wake."

Melinda Garcia aka Melinda NailFanatic is a modern-day renaissance woman. She possesses many skills and talents that she loves to share with her brothers and sisters of humanity. She offers high fashion nail services with unique and custom designs, intuitive tarot card readings, abstract paintings, drawings, and various mixed media visual arts. She designs clothing, jewelry and custom made furniture. Her use of color is astounding as she is color blind yet able to create vibrantly colorful masterpieces. To connect with and find out more about Melinda and her energy of **L**ove, **P**eace and **H**appiness, visit LPHtarot.com and NailFads.com.

Printed in the United States
By Bookmasters